24

HOURS

OF

TRANSFORMATION

Jennifer L. Gibaldi

TABLE OF CONTENTS

TABLE OF CONTENTS

MESSAGE FROM THE AUTHOR

Recently I had the pleasure of participating in a 24-hour Poetry Marathon where I was given a prompt at the start of every hour. I then had one hour to create and submit a poem based on that prompt. It was my first time participating and let me tell you - it was certainly an experience!

There were a few points where I thought "what did I get myself into?" I had moments where I wanted to give up and call it quits. There may have even been moments where I became a bit punchy and delirious... but I pushed through and stayed committed. I proudly completed the challenge, submitting my last poem, after being awake for a full 24 hours.

I have taken those poems and arranged them carefully for you in this very special collection. Every prompt given during the challenge aligned with my soul, igniting different emotions deep within me. Each poem explores the beauty of transformation in its various forms: mental, spiritual, and physical, and I am happy to share the journey with you.

Enjoy!

THE UNKNOWN

The levels rise,

One by one.

Move fast to keep up,

For one small misstep drops you into the unknown.

With each level comes new faces,

New situations.

Think quick,

Or get left behind.

WORD VOMIT

How does one silence the mind anyway?

The thoughts pour out,

Steady stream,

Non-stop,

Like word vomit.

Coming so fast I barely have time to make connections -

Forgive me for the incoherent banter.

FATE

An unkindness soaring through the air,

Make their presence known,

Forewarning beware!

Wishing to be left alone,

You hurry through; too pressed to care.

In the distance arises dawn,

And the Ravens begin to appear.

You quicken your pace,

Looking in the direction from which they have flown,

And you say a little prayer.

For all the kindness you have shown,

You hope to be spared.

You look up to see him perched high on his throne,

Staring back with a glare,

You feel deep in your bones.

SMALL YET MIGHTY

Covered in green moss,

Laying in the cool water,

The stones float freely.

DEATH OF A FOREST

You follow the trail,

Quietly observing.

Taking in all the sights and sounds,

You close your eyes.

You capture the moment in your mind,

Recording every possible detail.

The quiet babbling of the brook,

The chirping of the crickets,

Exchanged for the chorusing of the cicadas.

How the wind feels against your face,

The leaves crunching beneath your feet.

How the cool crisp air smells of pine,

The full, thick trees begin to shed their dark, green cover.

A tear forms and slowly trickles down your cheek.

For with the beauty of the fall,

Comes the death of the forest.

FIELD ON FIRE

Large open field,

Leaves color of fire,

Crisp cold air.

A NIGHT FOR LOVE

The warmth of the fire,

The glow of the flames.

The crackle of the sticks,

Like they're calling my name.

The stary night sky,

So far above.

Sets a nice mood,

For an evening of love.

I grab my favorite blanket,

Lay it out on the sand.

Invite him to sit,

Then reach for his hand.

Expecting a spark,

I feel a bit foolish.

For nothing was there,

Leaving me to rethink my wish.

I let go of his hand,

Look him in the eye.

No words are needed,

I softly begin to cry.

He stands to leave,

No apology offered.

I bury my head in my hands,

The night's tone is now altered.

SETTLING

God did not really want THIS for me - did he?

Little by little,

I started to get my voice back.

My opinions,

My thoughts,

My strength,

MYSELF.

Finally free,

I can live MY life again.

I can hold out for what I want,

What I know I deserve.

And if I don't find it?

That's fine.

I'd rather spend the rest of my life alone and happy,

Then miserable because I settled.

WHAT IS LOVE ANYWAY?

When you're feeling down,

And not the best version of yourself,

Love is what picks you up.

When you've had a bad day,

And take it out on those around you,

Love is understanding.

When you're hurt,

And unable to care for yourself,

Love takes over.

Love is the hug that warms your heart,

The smile that lets you know things will be okay.

Love is the candy bar he knew you would like,

The call to say hi, simply because he was thinking of you.

Love is growing together.

Learning to fully give yourself to another person,

Without having any expectations in return.

Love is beautiful.

Love is a blessing.

Love is life.

MY COCOON

Never the pretty one,

Or the popular one,

I was made fun of often.

Teased for how I looked,

How I talked.

I became extremely self-conscious,

More aware of my appearance than I should have been.

At all times,

My hair was done,

Make-up on and nails freshly painted.

Yet,

I still always felt like that ugly, unpopular girl.

I didn't notice the guys paying attention to me,

The girls who wanted to hang out.

I was the caterpillar who had transformed into a beautiful butterfly.

TAKE NOTICE

Running from it all.

Once small and meek,

Watching as they pass.

Hiding in the shadows,

I cower alone -

Remaining unnoticed.

Now -

Brave,

Strong,

Fierce.

A force to be reckoned with,

I emerge from the shadows.

They take notice,

Now they are the ones running.

MY OWN PATH

I stare straight ahead reluctant.

I know I should follow the lines,

But my heart is telling me to go off course.

Create my own path.

The choices in life are not always black and white,

We need to learn it is okay to zig-zag.

What is so wrong if we do?

Will the world stop?

Will life cease to exist?

No.

On the contrary.

It will be better.

It will reign with beauty,

Ooze with style.

It will have color and distinction,

Drenched in seductive suggestion.

All because creative minds made their own paths.

WALLS

I see your words,

Hear your call.

I look to the left,

Look to the right.

No way out,

No escape.

Trapped,

Blocked in by this barricade -

How do I break free?

I try to yell,

But it's no use.

You can't hear me,

You don't notice.

Too wrapped up in the memes on your screen,

To see that life is moving on without you.

The power dying,

You finally move.

Pick your head up to see the world,

Only to find yourself alone,

Surrounded by nothing but the wall you built.

THE CLIMB

Dark, tiny, confined,

Barely able to reach out in front of me.

I look up to see a pinpoint of light and have hope.

Looking for a way out, I push forward.

Wall.

I run my fingers along the floor and feel a rock.

I place my foot on it as the air starts to thicken.

Clenching onto a jagged stone,

I pull myself up, praying it does not give way.

I breathe a sigh of relief for it is strong,

And I take one more step up.

I feel around again, this time finding a crevice.

I hold my breath as I place my hand inside.

Relieved the crevice was not otherwise occupied,

I take another step up.

The weight of my body becoming heavier

Over the next few maneuvers,

I start to feel weak.

I want to give up,

Let go,

And fall back to the bottom.

I take another breath.

WAIT!

It's different...

The air isn't as thick.

I close my eyes for a moment, and when I open them -

I can start to make out the bricks on the wall...

My strength comes back, and I begin climbing faster.

Every so often, my foot slips.

I stop,

Discouraged and afraid.

I look up and see the pinpoint light has now

Become the size of a basketball.

I close my eyes and take a deep breath.

Slow down!

It's not a race, I remind myself.

I open my eyes and continue.

The darkness fading away,

I can breathe easier.

Are those voices I hear?

Are they calling my name?

No,

Just silence.

Feeling alone again,

I want to give up.

I start to cry, ready to let go.

What's the point?

There's no end to this.

But then...

The light becomes blinding,

The air,

Pure.

Suddenly,

I feel hands grabbing, pulling.

Frightened,

I scream and start to fight back.

My eyes adjust to the new light, and I stop.

I collapse into the safety of the arms of my family and friends,

My loved ones who helped save me from the darkness.

FREE

Walls of glass,

Doors of iron,

Nothing can keep me from you.

Screams of fear,

Tears of shame,

Nothing can make me forget.

Splintered wood,

Deafening silence,

Nothing could prepare me.

The deafening silence,

From the tears of shame,

Break through the glass walls.

Finally, I am free.

VOICE OF TWO WORLDS

The scent of pine and autumn lay softly in the cool crisp air.

"Come with me."

His soft whisper mixes with the calls of nature,

Like a love song only I can hear.

He has a calming sense about him,

Making me feel at peace in his presence.

I take a step forward and the air turns stale and frigid.

"No. Stay here, with me."

His voice deep and raspy,

Sends a shudder through my spine.

I turn and look to see the cold darkness.

No longer is the scent of pine and autumn.

No longer do I hear the love song,

No longer am I at peace.

'He is right',

I start to think,

And take a step back.

"Come with me,"

The love song breaks through.

I pause and look forward,

To the calm openness.

I take a deep breath,

A sigh of relief.

As I take his hand,

I step forward into the open field of hopes and dreams.

POWER

How is it possible to have an opinion,

An original thought,

When you are being silenced?

How can one express themselves,

Openly and honestly,

When being weighed down?

We are encouraged to:

Think for yourself -

Speak your mind!

And when we do?

Oh, no -

Not like that...

Now what?

Do we comply,

Like good little puppets?

Or do we fight?

Take off the muzzles,

Remove the weights -

TAKE BACK YOUR POWER!

COME WITH ME, MY CHILD

I stand alone,

Victim to my own thoughts,

Surrounded by darkness.

Wanting to move forward,

Step out of this vast emptiness,

I look around.

Prisoner to the situation,

Bystander to life.

Thinking about the what-if,

Wishing it were different,

I break free.

No longer a victim,

No longer a prisoner.

Shifting into the light,

Creating a new path,

I have evolved.

MY ZEN

The cool morning air against my face,

The chirping of the crickets, my only companion.

I am at peace in my happy place,

Full of serenity and tranquility.

With each step I take,

I become lighter as the stress melts away.

By the time I reach my front door,

I am floating on air.

Calm,

Focused,

Centered.

Ready to take on the day.

HOPE

Through the fog I can see the light,

Filtering in like a rainbow of lasers.

My heart starts to lift,

No longer a sinking feeling in my chest.

I close my eyes,

Inhale deeply,

I am at peace.

The worries of yesterday gone,

The promise of tomorrow taking its place.

KALEIDOSCOPE OF LIFE

Life is ever-changing.

With each different path taken,

A new view emerges.

And we converge,

Trying to see,

The new vision that has come to be.

Steady is the hand that passes,

This ever-changing form of ashes.

Like looking through a Kaleidoscope,

Your heart begins to fill with hope.

All the intricate shapes and bright colors,

You move around, praying to find others.

Only to reach the last lonely stop,

Where you lost your Kaleidoscope and felt your heart drop.

THIS MOMENT

"Push me, Daddy!"

"Higher."

"HIGHER!"

The giggles are loud and infectious as my toes touch the sky.

The colors swirl around me, becoming one as I fly through them.

Knowing he is behind me,

I live in the moment, enjoying the thrill.

"Push me, Daddy!"

"Higher."

I smile ear-to-ear as my toes graze the tops of the fields.

The steady colors lining my vision.

Knowing he is behind me,

I enjoy the moment.

"Push me, Daddy!"

I close my eyes and smile, as my toes scrape across the ground.

The colorful flowers sitting on the side.

Knowing he is behind me,

I treasure the moment.

"Push me, Baby Girl."

His smile is warm as he picks up his feet.

The touch of his hand comforting, as he places it on mine.

And knowing I am behind him,

I thank God for this moment.

ONE DAY

Answer the phone when they call.

Take the time to say I love you too.

Let them hold on a little longer when they hug you.

Because one day...

Laugh at their lame jokes.

Listen when they tell the same story for the hundredth time.

Appreciate the advice and wisdom they have to offer.

Because one day...

Let them pay.

Take the pictures,

Visit with them.

Because one day...

One day, the phone will no longer ring.

There will be no more I love yous, no more hugs.

The stories will have ended,

There will be no more advice.

One day,

You will be left with nothing,

Except the pictures and the memories.

FINAL EXAM

I would like to start by Congratulating you all on making it this far - Welcome to your final exam!

This exam is made up of the following three parts:

- 20 multiple choice questions on relationship interactions

- 20 short answer questions on your childhood hopes and dreams

- 1 500-word essay on self-reflection

Not only will you be tested on your knowledge of the material,

But also,

How you are effectively able to apply it in your day-to-day living -

As well as your ability to adapt and change,

When the unexpected occurs.

You have 1 hour to show your worth,

Plead your case, and fully prove yourself.

You will be graded based upon someone else's opinion of you,

And your results will be used to determine

Where your journey will take you from here.

Good luck to you all,

You may start …

Now!

ABOUT THE AUTHOR

Jennifer Gibaldi is an upcoming poet and author. She has recently published her first collection of poems *Perfectly Imperfect*, available on Amazon.com, where she brings you along on her journey of obstacles that she has faced over the years and shares how she has coped with them.

Jennifer is currently working on her third poetry collection, as well as a debut novel. She draws on her real-life experiences for inspiration, writing with pure heart and raw emotion. She looks forward to sharing her story with the world in hopes that she can comfort and inspire those who are in similar situations.

Jennifer can be found performing at various open mics throughout Long Island New York. You can follow her on Instagram @iamworthit82 and her Facebook author page I AM Worth It.